CH00879946

SOME WORDS BURN BRIGHTLY

AN ILLUMINATED POETRY COLLECTION

MARY E. LOWD

———

Copyright © 2023 by Mary E. Lowd

All rights reserved.

No part of this book may be reproduced in any form or by any electronic or mechanical means, including information storage and retrieval systems, without written permission from the author, except for the use of brief quotations in a book review.

Art deco divider is designed by Freepik.

For my mother, who read poetry to me as a child, whether I wanted her to or not.

And for all the people who make beautiful things to share with the world, simply for the sake of sharing them.

CONTENTS

PREFACE

I never considered myself a poet. Since I was a child, I was a writer. I wanted to write long series of novels, and I scorned anything as short as a mere short story. Poems were right out. But when I began taking my writing seriously after college, I followed the common advice at the time and started with short stories, not because I liked them but because they were a good way to practice and build my skills. Over the years, I developed a taste for short stories, but I still scorned most poetry. Or at least, I thought I did.

My mother read poems to me as a child. I have no idea how many times she read T. S. Eliot's "The Love Song of J. Alfred Prufrock" or e. e. cummings' "here is little Effie's head" to me. Certainly, enough times for me to memorize large portions of them without realizing it until much later. I studied poetry as I got my English degree in college—the class I took on John Milton was life-changing, and I still frequently think about the class I took on Modernist Poetry twenty years later.

I never thought of myself as a poet. I didn't even think I liked poetry. But I read a lot of it. I thought about it a lot. I certainly had favorites—I've always loved William Wordsworth's "I Wandered Lonely as Cloud" and essentially every poem ever written by Stephen Crane. And when an idea struck me, sometimes I would write a poem down, just to get it out of my head. Usually, my poems were inspired by photographs I took of the flowers in my garden—primarily daffodils, which are my favorite, and roses. I would write poems that followed the arc of the year, describing my favorite flowers as they aged through the seasons.

Then the pandemic struck in 2020, and I found myself relating to the outside world almost entirely through social media. I started writing poems in response to nature photographs taken by other people who were kind enough to post their pictures online for others to see. They brought beauty to me, and alone and isolated in the middle of the night (usually), huddling over my computer (always), I tried to thank them by writing little poems inspired by their photographs. Most of the nature photographs that inspired me during this time were of adorable animals.

Fast forward another couple years, and I found myself, as I approached my 41st birthday, thinking about the power of single phrases. Sometimes, a few words can stay with you longer than an entire novel. And I think, that is the heart of poetry. A few words with so much power that they stay with you, echoing in your head, as entire seasons of your life pass. I looked back at the poems I'd written—which had felt like frivolous little fripperies at the time—and I realized, some of those poems had kept echoing inside my head for longer than anything in the dozen or so novels I've written.

I pulled all those poems about flowers and animals together, rescuing many of them from disappearing into the black hole of social media—poems I'd been amassing for more than twenty years—and discovered that while I thought I'd scorned poetry, I had written an entire poetry book. And furthermore, I believe it's a book I would have loved as a child, before I forgot how to see the magic in poetry.

I've discovered the magic of poetry again, and if you'll let me, dear reader, I would like to share it with you.

PART I
NATURE

ALBEDO EFFECT

The traces we leave behind...

Just by being there,
You can collect warmth
Without knowing it,
Affecting the world
Around you, and
Leaving an imprint
Of the space you fill.

HIDDEN LOVE

When the trees hold the moon
In their branches
At night
Twigs becomes fingers
In mere phantom touches
Their caresses reluctant
For what if the moon saw their love?
What if the moon didn't requite?

Trees reach with longing
Their love simply becoming
A haunting, beautiful sight

IMPLICATION

There must be a giant tree next door
Covered in blossoms
Because tiny white flower petals
Drift through my yard
And I see them through the window

A tree is implied

THE FAIRY FLOWER

Her wings askew
Like petals gold
The fairy's flight
From love withheld
Freezes her

Statue still; statue cold
Yet spring's delight
Warm sap like blood
Enlivens her

And stillness softens
Coldness yields
Like nymphs of old
No longer fairy
She becomes a flower in the field

THE GORGON FLOWER

Three roses share one stem,
Like three crones share one eye.

Steal their stem,
Like Perseus stole the eye,
And your treasure,
The roses will become.

Unless, like Gorgons,
They turn you into stone.

Pick the flowers,
At your own peril.

WHAT THE THIRD EYE SEES

Wings of light,
A ruffled dress,
Faeries flight,
Under the sun's caress.

Flower or fae,
Who can say?
Only the third eye sees,
The truth in fancy's flight.

THE YELLOW ROSEBUD

The yellow rosebud holds a secret in its petals,
Like a promise,
On the tip of the tongue,
Unspoken,
Uncertain,
Waiting for the moment when trust blooms,
And the words can finally be said.

THE YELLOW ROSE DREAMS

The rose turns her yellow face
Open and vulnerable
Toward the yellow face
Of the sun
And dreams
The star looks back at her.

TWO ROSES

Two roses—
The full rose, petals pale with age,
The rosebud, petals bright with youth,
—both perfect, in their way.

THE LATE AUGUST ROSE

The late August rose,
Has seen the summer passing.
Petals fall from its blooms,
Like scales from our eyes.

Stare into the future,
Like the rose.
Unflinching,
Braced with thorns,
But with open eyes,
And arms wide,
Anyway.

THE NOVEMBER ROSE

The November rose
Doesn't care about the time
Or weather or
The growing darkness
All around

The November rose is here
And shines like the sunrise
Glowing softly
For the sheer love

Of being

THE EARLY DAFFODIL

Be brave,
Little daffodil;
The cold
won't last.

LEMON BUTTER STAR

Lemon butter star,
Shining from the earth,
Full of flavor,
Full of light,
When we wonder who we are,
What anything is worth,
As least we can savor,

The simple daffodil,

And hold its beauty tight,
Against the pressures of a long, long night.

GOLDEN TRUMPETS

Every spring,
My heart recites
A haiku at this sight:

Yellow stars in the grass;
Golden trumpets,
Herald the coming of spring!

Their brassy beat,
My heart's lyric,
A song together,
Of sight
And mind.

YELLOW STARS

Bright yellow stars,
A constellation of daffodils,
Bobbing in the breeze,
In my front yard.

SIMPLE COMPANIONSHIP

Two flowers beside each other,
Without words or needs,

Swaying in the same breeze,
Shaded by the same clouds,
Glowing under the same sun—

This is companionship,
As simple as it comes.

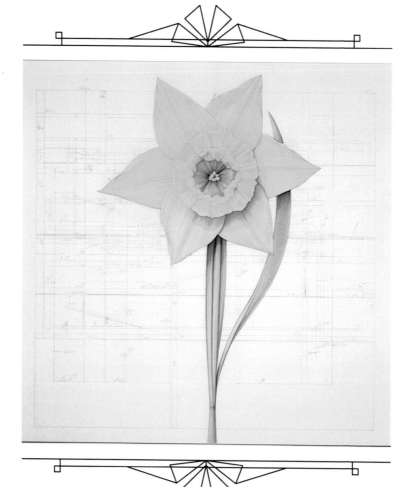

BLUEPRINT FOR A DAFFODIL

The architecture of the daffodil
Fascinates me

Every curve and contour
So bold and exact

The same every year
From flower to flower
Across the seasons of a life
They grow the same
While we all change

They are memories reborn
Memories relived
New memories made

All in a flower

PART II
CATS

FLOWERS AND CATS

Bouquets of flowers
Bouquets of cats
Arranged in rows
Arranged in vats

Which is prettier?
Who can know

Golden daffodil
Or black feline
Laid out, divine
Sunning in a windowsill?

TUXEDO CAT

Black, white & mysterious
Traveling through a field
You see something curious

A fine feline
Dressed to the nines
In a tuxedo
Surrounded by Queen Anne's lace

Perched on a pole
What secrets might a cat know?

Stay awhile beside 'em
Mayhap they'll decide
To share a secret or two

BLACK CAT IN MOTION

Among jungle greens
With eyes so keen
Passed a silky black cat

Slipping through daylight
A shadow come to life
This feline's grace
Has no time to waste

When disturbed—
Oh so perturbed!
The beautiful feline
Very rudely spat

Hissing to say:
Get out of my way
You fool, now scat!

BLACK CAT IN STILLNESS

Dark, round & weighty
Silky, black & velvety
Can anyone escape?

Beware, if you traipse
Too close to this
Gravitational pull
This soothing purr—

A whole world
Of love & warmth & coy
Feline graces—

When caught in its embraces
You may ne'er leave
But oh what joy
Ye shall receive!

THE ORANGE CAT

The sun in the sky,
Cannot shine more brightly,
Than an orange cat's glow,
When she knows,
She's the most glorious fellow,
Ever to be seen,
On a field of green.

TWO CATS

Back to back
Cat to cat
Secrets pass
They're on the lookout
Guarding against what?
Know one knows
Except the cats
Who will always have
Each other's backs

THE CAT AND THE CHAIR

If to arise you desire
Without earning my ire
Then answer thee
These riddles three...

Why are you a fool?
How are you such a fool?
When will this foolishness end?

Your answers are wrong
Now sing me a song
As you play the part of a chair
I have been more than fair

GOLDEN EYES

The gold burns brightly
Taking time nightly
To stare through your heart
Pierce you suddenly, with a start

How can a simple feline
Have eyes so divine?

THOSE EYES

Sunken eyes
Carved in a face
Soft and grey

Is it wise
To stare in those eyes
Or will this specter

—A feline, feeling neglected
Hungry and haunting
Filled with wanting—

Steal your soul away?

GREEN EYES

Green fire
Expressing ire
And perhaps
A latent desire

If gazing could invoke
The viewer to gently stroke
Behind this feline's ears
The gesture might endear
A lowly human to the graces
Of a member of such a godly species

THE CAT AND THE BOX

Silky black
Like the night sky without stars
Or the depths of a cave without torches
The cat's fur gleams

Wrapped in paper
Swaddled in cardboard
This wonderful package
Awaits

No uncertainty here
No experiment in quantum physics
Just a cat

In a box

THE CAT AND THE BIRDHOUSE

Wait for the birds
Where they're sure to come
Home to roost

Crouch in a house
Much too small
Knowing you have but to wait

The birds will come
Surely they'll come?

The cat in the birdhouse
Has only to wait
And wait
And wait

PUDDLE PORTAL

What is this?
What is this?
No mere mud puddle!
Not to be understood by you,
Mere mortal!

Only the glowing eyes
Of a knowing cat
Can see
Deeply enough to divine
A path to other worlds so fine
Hidden in the murky water

A shimmering portal!

Now if only
Splashing paws can find it

THE KITTEN AND A STREAM OF WATER

The drip, drip, dripping
Of the faucet
Draws the interest
Of this small cat
Bat, bat, batting at the stream
It is not what it seems—
Can't be caught with claws
Nor crushed with jaws—
Mysterious string
Wondrous thing
Baffling and cool

Making cats into fools

KITTEN BECOMES CAT

Fuzzy kitten
Small and sweet
Tiny ears and tiny feet

Give it time
And kittens grow
So, so fast
Faster than you know

Now there's a cat
Where the kitten was

It's enough to give one pause

Longer tail and fluffier fur
But deep inside
Beats the same heart as before

INDOOR CAT

Oh cruel glass,
Doth block the way,
Tween youthful cat,
And yonder play.

What shall a cat do?
So sadly restrained...
Climb and claw!
Never be tamed!

PART III
DOGS

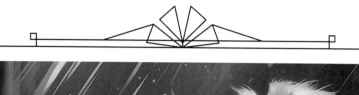

SNOW DAY

Dogs and snow!
On adventures they will go!
Roll in powder,
Taste the flakes,
Staying inside today,
Would be a great mistake.

Except the cat knows,
It's warm inside,
With fires and cushions to enjoy,
The perfect cozy place to hide.

THE DOG AND THE MUDDY LAKE

I.

Great and grand
This dog would stand
But stretched beside a lake
It did repose
A playful roll
And plop!

The dog did fall
Right into the drink
Not deep enough to sink
Just a blow
To dignity
Is all
But what is dignity?
When a dog can play?

So up it gets!
And off it goes

2.

One big mud puddle
Where one big pup muddles
Sloshing in the dirty water
With a big grin on their face
Not trying to win any race

It gives the mind fodder
How one might get farther
Choosing to emulate
A happy, soggy dog
Than chasing after fate

SUPERHERO DOG

Sleeping soundly,
Like a log,
This good dog,
Flies through skies,
Rich with clouds,

O'er stars and rainbows,
Their four paws bound,

Down to sleep they go,
Then like a superhero,
Up through dreams, they rise.

THE DOG INTERVIEW

No one likes to be interviewed
Not even a dog
So grumbling and whining
Trying not to be rude
The hopeful candidate
Wades through this slog

At the end will they rate?
Will they want the job?

A tell-tale wag
A beard-hidden grin
Though not one to brag
A new home is quite a win

SNOW DOG

The sun's a star
Its light from the sky
Glitters over ice
Morning is nigh

Two ears emerge
Mere triangles
Twin tiny summits
Peaking up from the ground

Give them time
To grow and enlarge
Below the snow
A dog grows ready
For their first BARK!

Snow finally melts
Huskies abound!

WINTER FOLLOWS SPRING

The big white dogs of winter
The small black goats of spring

The dogs stand alert and waiting
Until the goats come hopping
And lead the way
To longer days
And sunnier skies

Winter and spring
Together sing
Waiting for summer to rise

PART IV
ANIMALS

SHEEP

The shy sheep peers
Between branches of the tree
Holding back its ears
Wondering and wanting
The bravery for asking
A question so bashful
Cautious and tactful
They just want to know, you see
"Will you be friends with me?"

THREE DEER

1.
Three deer
Reflected in a pool
The sky behind them
As colorful as a jewel
The day is theirs
Nighttime too
Three friends
With time to share
And time to spend

2.
A red deer stands
Silhouetted and still
The blue sky frames its pose
Like a picture on a windowsill

The sounds of evening
Fill the deer's ready ears
Perhaps birds singing
Perhaps something the deer fears

Will it run?
Or stay and graze?
All we can do is watch
with a steady gaze

3.
They have to be cautious
In case someone is watching
But three roe deer
Dancing & prancing
Right after sunset
Playing & jumping...
Until they're unsettled
Sniffing on the wind
Just a whiff in the wind
Yes, someone is watching
And they must attend
To their fears
These three deer

FOUR HORSES

Four horses on a grey and gloomy day,
Stop to drink some water on their way,
Shall they ride to battle?
Shall they ride to glory?

Perhaps they'll simply wander,
Hooves sloshing marshes,
Letting their equine souls ponder,
Letting their hearts have the final say.

HEDGEHOG HIGHWAY

Travelin' along,
Prickly and fine,
Singin' a song,
Of how the road will be mine.

Takin' a journey,
Into the unknown,
No matter what they say,
Gonna keep on waddlin',
Down the Hedgehog Highway.

HEDGEHOG FEAST

Mangoes, strawberries, orange, and bell pepper
A veritable rainbow of fruit to share
But what is this?
All round and prickly?
Covered in spines so stickly?
Not a fruit
This funny dude
Is a guest
So be aware
And don't you dare
Hog the treats
Until this hedgehog eats
Their share

PYGMY MARMOSET

With the round face of an owl
Tiny hands & tiny tail
The pygmy marmoset
Is all set
To dig in

One green grape is the size
Of a watermelon
To these little eyes
Hungry maw
And rumbling belly

Munch away, little one
Eat to your heart's content

A whole feast in a bunch of grapes

VOLE

As small as an apple
This vole samples
Seeds and grains and scraps
Not worrying about any traps

Living its small life
Avoiding any strife
Just going about the day
Not getting in anyone's way

ECHIDNA

Spiny backed
And pointy nosed
Toddling along
Wherever it goes

Not a hedgehog
Not a bird
Though it lays eggs
And is covered in quills

What is this creature
With such strange features?

The echidna knows

MOLE

What is this thing?
Dirty brown and blunt clawed,
Stubby nosed and pink pawed,
Velvet fur,
Winking eyes,
I must surmise,
'Tis a mole,
At the surface and unsure,
Of where to go.

FOX IN MOTION

Seek and you may find
A blaze of red
Quick and bright
Darting o'er the grass

A fox, dancing
Your heart, singing

A balm to the mind
It may be said
Seeing such a sight
Though 'tis over in a flash

FOX IN STILLNESS

Foxes in parables
Are always clever fools
Tricking and taunting
Winning their way

But sometimes a fox
Gets just what they want
By sitting and sunning
In a green field all day

RACCOONS

Heists and capers
This pack of bandits
Is at the ready
Already dressed
Masks o'er faces
Rings around tails
They'll run rings around you

Scaling walls
Climbing ladders
You're definitely not ready
For all their devious
Paw print covered
Blueprints
Plans
And clever scams

QUOKKA

Angry animals,
Glaring at you,
From every direction,
Making you wonder:
What did you do?
To earn their ire?

But then a friend!
A happy face!
The quokka is glad,
You're in this place,
And smiles and smiles,
Sharing with all,
Their joyful inner fire.

RED PANDA

Sleeping in a tree,
Cozy as can be,
Squished between branches,
This red panda dances,
Through dreams,
And visions,
We can't see.

THE LION AND THE TURTLE

The lion stops
For a simple drink
A pause in his day
A moment to think

But alas!
An interruption!
A sudden eruption
From the water
A turtle declares
"This pond is mine!"

The king of the jungle withdraws
As would any civilized lion

HIPPO

Oh, hippo!
Lo and behold, hippo!
Thou art so small
No taller art thou
Than a Wellington boot

Forsooth!
No time can be wasted
When your presence graced it
New to the world
So tiny
And so cute

WHALE

Bulbous blimp
Ridiculous thing
Breasting waves
Swimming with fins

Where did it come from?
How did it come to be?
Long ago,
Don't you know?
They left the land
Gave up their hooves

Now only lingering
Remnants remain
Of their old ungulate frames
As underwater
They do sing.

THE UNKNOWABLE MIND OF A FROG

A pair of eyes,
A glassy mirror,
What lurks beneath?

Kicking legs,
Webbed feet,
The steady breaths...

And unknowable thoughts,
Inside the mind of a frog.

POND BREAK

The haunting strains of a jazzy song
Deep in the green water
Where newts belong
Wishing and swishing
Swimming and brimming
With wiggly tails
Of salamanders
Who know the peace
Of life beneath
A glassy roof

Stay awhile
And just look

PART V
BIRDS

STARLINGS LIKE STARS

1.
One bird
Swooping over the ocean

One bird
Only one
But each feather
Each single feather
Is another
And another
More birds than can be counted
When all is accounted for
When all is done

The starlings fly together
Each bird
A tiny part
Of the bigger one

2.
Starlings like stars

Flitting and flying
Filling the powder blue
With their plentitude

As thick as galaxies
Dense as nebulae
But not so far away
They fill our sky
On this side
Of the horizon
Inside the sphere
Where we all live

Stars within reach
Starlings
Like stars

3.
Red giants and white dwarfs,
Scattered through the sky,
Deep black fields of velvet,
Purple dusty swirls,
The entire cosmos,
In the feathers,
Of one,
Beautiful,
Bird.

BLACK-BELLIED DIPPER

Small black bird
With a bright white breast
Flitting through the forest
Living by a stream
You could walk for hours
Not speaking a single word

Just to catch a glimpse
Of this brilliantly colored
Black and white bird

When, at last, you find it
What a treasure it will seem!

NORTHERN FLICKER

1.

Yellow breasted
With a black moon collar
Speckled and proud

Though you try to get rested
A giggling holler
Knocking and drumming
Keep you from sleeping

Some birds are loud

2.

Red headed
Green backed
Sharp beaked
Give me some slack

So I peck on wood
Make lots of noise
But a beautiful bird
Is one of life's great joys

SOUTH ISLAND TAKAHĒ

Round as the world
Blue as the sea
Its wings are furled
And it's staring at me

Bright orange eye
And a serious beak
Travel through time
Only to seek
A forgotten species
Thought extinct
Now right here
Round as a sphere

EGRET

The egret wanders
Through the waters
Snacking as it goes
Its white plumage shows
Sunlight and shadows
Playing so brightly
Across its back
It has the knack
Strutting as confidently
As any waterfowl
Living its life
In the here and now

A PUFFIN NESTING

Birds fill the air,
Like tufts of dandelion down,
Soaring and swooping by the sea,

But on the rocky shore,
One bird, face painted like a clown,
Does not fly free,
Toiling away,
Planning for future days,
The puffin makes a nest,
Where someday, eggs will rest.

OWL

Fuzzy & funny
The owl skews an eye
Giving a quizzical look

The Wise One wonders
Why you choose to reside
Trapped inside
A big wood box
When the sky stretches wide
With room to fly
Space for wings
Wandering thoughts
And wondering things

Perhaps that's why—
Oh, poor Wingless One!

PART VI
WHIMSY

THE OTTER IN THE LILAC BUSH

I.

As I wandered on a sunny day,
I came upon an otter along my way,
Living in a lilac bush.

"What news?" asked I,
And he did say,
"I am an otter in a lilac bush.

"For news ask badgers,
"For songs ask birds.

"I am an otter,
"And all I offer to travelers along the way is a single
    word."

2.

"Hide!" he said and ran away,

I chased that otter on a sunny day,
And found him hidden behind a rose so orange.

"Why?" asked I, but away he ran,
Leaving nothing but the rose and me.

A rose is good company,
But the otter's behavior did intrigue,
And I gave chase as best I can.

3.

Next I found the otter,
Looking for all the world,
Like a fairy with her wings unfurled.

Purple wings,
An iris sings with color not with words.

"You see me?" the otter asked,
And I answered plain and true.

Away he scurried;
It seemed our chase was not yet through.

4.

The otter scurried,
I followed faithful,
From purple iris to yellow rose.

He stuck his nose amid the petals,
I followed suit & followed him.
From rose to rose we ran.

Each rose smelled sweet,
With each sniff he smiled,
'Twas a better way to pass a while,
Than any other I can ken.

5.

I met an otter in a lilac bush,
& spent the day chasing him,

From flower to flower,
We toured the grounds,

Running & stopping,
Chasing & hiding,
Under the summer sun.

Flowers speak in color,
Birds speak in song,

My otter spoke few words,
But made the world turn round with fun.

THE OTTER AND THE DAFFODILS

1.

An otter went walking in the woods one day,
And saw some yellow flowers along the way,
"I have friends who'd like to see," quoth he,
"These yellow flowers in a picture with me!"

2.

Standing underneath the daffodil tree,
Just an otter waiting to see what he can see,
You say you don't think "daffodil" is a kind of tree?
Well, says the otter, it's taller than me!

3.

Oh, when the sun comes up & shines on the flowers
    without a care
And there's nothing you'd rather do than stroll along on
    a day so fair
Under the daffodils, walking along the way
Under the daffodils, having a very fine day
Oh, under the daffodils, an otter awaits you there

THE OTTER AND THE ROSE

1.

An otter and a rose,
Enjoy the sunset together—
Trading secrets,
Sharing dreams,
Whispering words,
That get carried away by the wind.

2.

Under an arch of flowers,
A handsome otter
Tells you an important secret.

Only you know
What it is.

THE OTTER AND THE NEIGHING FLOWERS

At the vanguard of the flowers,
"Charge!" cries the otter,
"Bring joy and color to the world!"

"Nay!" cry the flowers,
"We are not a battalion!"

"Neigh?!?" asks the otter,
"Are you horses to answer so?"

"Mayhap," say the flowers,
And continue lounging in their field.

THE FAIRY STEED

In a fairyland of flowers
Under the thick, streaming sun
Stands a fairy rider
Aching for some fun

Here comes a jolly steed!
A faithful dog
Jovial & true
To save the day
Carrying the rider away
Through fields & dales
Meadows & vales...

Oh, without a corgi
What would a fairy do?

THE CAT WHO WISHED TO BE A HORSE

Come join the hunt!
Gallop & trot
Whinny & neigh
And if your whinny
Sounds more like meow...
Don't let it get in the way!

We're all strong horses
Noble & true
Even the few of us
Whose eyes glow at night
And tails swish at the sight
Of a mouse
Plump & fair...
But don't you dare

Say a cat doesn't belong
For you're wrong
A galloping cat
Has every right
To stride through the night

Hunting beside horses so fine
With their riders astride...

Wait a minute

Riders?
Astride?
Never mind

Cats hunt alone
Now where was that mouse?
I'll soon make it my own

THE NECROMOUSER CYCLE

I.
Like a cat,
I bring you a dead mouse,
Mine has ellipses for a tail.........

II.
Make me a necromancer!
Be my lightning machine,
Resurrect this poem many times,
In your eyes and mind.

III.
Little mousies,
Eating Orchids,
But mousies don't eat orchids,
So this poem isn't true.

DO YOU DARE?

When the mighty peach doth approacheth,
Wield thy vorpal cats and their snicky-snacky claws,
All twill be avenged upon such floral spheres,
They were ne'er giants nor windmills,
Only the fruit of nonsense upon a platter.
So, slay yon peach!
And, with the owl's runcible spoon,
Serve it to thy loyal cats, brave cats.
They will disdain it. But you may feast,
Knowing that no peach — so sweet,
and so cold — shall ever defeat thee.
So much depends upon it. And a wheelbarrow.

PART VII
THOUGHTS

THE DESERT SUN MARKS
A DAY

Low in the sky,
Surrounded by a pink haze,
The sun stares lazily out at me,

Rising higher,
The sky grows bluer,
And the sun blazes bright,

Back to pink,
On comes the night,

The desert cycles through a day,
Clear, warm, aglow,
Staving off thoughts of snow,
Far away.

A COMMON SUNSET

A sunset is
More common
Than an eclipse,

But arguably
Just as stunning.

We live under
A beautiful star.

WAITING ON ELAINE

Before a daughter, a time of waiting,
A time before memory.
I walk the halls of my own childhood,
Places and houses only dimly remembered;
I will not find her there
But I think I am looking.

My Uncle's house; the house on Garfield St.
Places I lived before I lived,
When I mainly lived in another's eyes,
As she lives in this empty house.

Now is the time and place before her memory.
Even after the waiting; even when she is here,
This house will have the quality not only of a dream
But of the fading memory of a dream.
To her.

Like Garfield St.
And my Uncle's house to me.

In these places and times, known mostly vicariously,
Perhaps subconsciously, on the edge of our beings,
Before she is my daughter and I am a mother,
Instead we are infants, daughters together,

Proto-minds struggling and reaching,
Waiting to wake up and discover,
In the future, our own selves.

IN THE ROOM

The voices in the room
Criss-crossing
Over, under
Each other

Speaking of hope & doom
How to think
Who is right
All through the night

Never ceasing
Unrelenting—

For a moment
A connection
Two minds meet
Not necessarily to agree
But seeing each other
A small wonder

& that is why

THE SWEET BERRY

A wise Sage walked in a yard
Eating of the berries that there grew,
They tempted with color black,
They taunted with taste
Sour as were they green.
The Sage ate unheedingly.

Finishing of her turpentine supper,
The sage, triumphant, announced
"The world is benevolent, the last berry is ripe."

Walking away content, she found a thorn in her sandal.

BROKEN SHELLS

The ocean waves
Wash over
The broken shells,
Singing
Like wind chimes.

BETWEEN THE WAVES

Life is like
Building a sandcastle
As the tide comes in.

Eventually everything you do
Will be washed away,
But sometimes,
Between the waves,

Your work stands sentinel,

Glittering and gold
Beside
The sea.

SOME WORDS BURN BRIGHTLY

Can a few words burn brightly enough
To light all the seasons
Of a life?

Which words?
How do we find them?

This is why we read

We're alway searching, searching
Through books and pages
Streams of words
And sudden downpours
For the few words
That glow
For the words that cast light
On the things we see

Some words are lanterns
Carried with us
Clung to tightly

Some words are sudden sunbreaks
Momentary enlightenment
That soon fades away
But leaves a memory of what
Was seen

Some words rise like the sun
And illuminate your world
For a season
For a day
A year

A life?

Some words are a guiding star
Some words last a whole life long
Or longer

Some words fade away
But some words...

Some words last

ABOUT THE AUTHOR

Mary E. Lowd is a prolific science-fiction and furry writer in Oregon. She's had more than 200 short stories and a dozen novels published, always with more on the way. Her work has won three Ursa Major Awards, ten Leo Literary Awards, and four Cóyotl Awards. She edited FurPlanet's ROAR anthology series for five years, and she is now the editor and founder of the furry e-zine *Zooscape*. She lives in a crashed spaceship, disguised as a house and hidden behind a rose garden, with an extensive menagerie of animals, some real and some imaginary.

For more information:
marylowd.com

To read Mary's short stories:
deepskyanchor.com

ALSO BY MARY E. LOWD

Otters In Space

Otters In Space 2: Jupiter, Deadly

Otters In Space 3: Octopus Ascending

In a Dog's World

Jove Deadly's Lunar Detective Agency

The Necromouser and Other Magical Cats

You're Cordially Invited to Crossroads Station

Queen Hazel and Beloved Beverly

Tri-Galactic Trek

Nexus Nine

The Celestial Fragments (A Labyrinth of Souls Trilogy)

The Snake's Song

The Bee's Waltz

The Otter's Wings

The Entangled Universe

Entanglement Bound

The Entropy Fountain

Starwhal in Flight

Xeno-Spectre

Hell Moon

The Ancient Egg

Milton Keynes UK
Ingram Content Group UK Ltd.
UKRC030134171123
432729UK00005B/87

* 9 7 8 1 0 8 8 0 5 7 4 8 3 *